Paleo Canning
Tips and Tricks including
25 Easy and Delicious Recipes

Contents

Paleo Canning.. 1

Tips and Tricks including... 1

25 Easy and Delicious Recipes.. 1

Introduction 5

Methods in canning: 7

Canning Equipment... 7

    Water bath canner 7

    Pressure canners.. 7

Meat, chicken and seafood recipes 9

    Beef stew... 9

    Chicken soup 10

    Salmon or shad... 11

Vegetable recipes 12

    Pickled asparagus 12

    Turkish fermented cabbage 13

    Pickled beets 14

    Pickled dill carrots... 15

    Spiced pickled carrots.. 16

    Pickled cauliflower 17

    Vietnamese carrot and radish pickle.................................... 18

    Radish relish... 19

    Jams, Jellies and Marmalades 20

    Apple and earl grey almond jelly... 21

    Banana jam 22

    Banana and passion fruit jam 23

    Money butter... 24

Cranberry orange jelly 25

Blueberry jam 26

Blackberry jam 27

Golden raspberry jam 28

Pear preserves 29

Pie Fillings 30

Blackberry pie filling 31

Peach blueberry pie filling 32

Canning Tips and Tricks 33

Extend the shelf life of your preserves 33

Tips for making a good marmalade 33

How to be creative and still be safe 33

How to save runny jam 33

How to prevent jar breakage 34

How to store your canned jars 34

What to do if black scum forms outside the jars 34

How to throw away spoils 35

Importance of labeling jars 35

Air bubbles in your jars 35

How to check the seal of the jars 35

Next Steps 37

Introduction

Back when most families depended on fresh produce harvested on their own garden for food, preserving it became a necessity to prolong its shelf life. This also allowed families to enjoy food that are currently out of season.

It is common to see canning jars filled with colorful jellies and fruits in stores and even farmer's markets. Some people even have their own canning recipe which has been passed down to them from by their ancestors. People have different reasons why they preserve food through the canning method but here are some of the benefits derived in the process:

- Health. Making your own canned food enables you to know exactly what is in it. You can avoid preservatives and other additives found in commercially produced canned food by making your own.

- Eco-friendly. You can limit food waste by canning your excess produce. Remember that the mason jars used in canning is also reusable so you do not have to use and discard jars every time you make preserves.

- Financial. Purchasing fruits and vegetables when they are in season enables you to save money. Also, you can create your own jams and jellies for your breakfast for a quarter of the price.

- Sentimental reasons. Some families pass on the canning recipe from parent to child. This makes people feel that they are continuing a family legacy whenever they prepare canned foods.

- Preserve personal harvest. People with backyard gardens can preserve excess produce and reduce waste.

- Gifts. Canned foods can be a good gift idea most especially if the receiver has already tasted your recipe. Having several cans ready can also be helpful when you need to give gift unexpectedly.

- Quality and taste. The best tasting canned food are those that are locally grown and harvested in season. It is very satisfying and rewarding to select your own ingredients for the recipes.

Paleo canning recipes enable people to preserve organic produce while adhering to the basic principles of the diet.

Canning is a preservation technique that aims to maintain the flavor of the fruit or vegetable. It is a safe method of packing jars with food and placing them in high temperature to kill any bacteria and organism that can cause it to spoil. Air is also forced out of the jar and a vacuum seal is created once the preserve starts to cool. This vacuum protects the food from being contaminated by microorganisms.

Methods in canning:

There are generally two ways to preserve food: water bath method and the pressure canner method.

Boiling water method is used for fruits, tomatoes and even pickle. The jars are submerged in boiling water and cooked for a predetermined amount of time. Pressure canning is considered as the only safe way to preserve vegetables, seafood, poultry and meats. The jars are placed in a cooker with 3 inches of water and it is heated at 240 degrees.

This is essential because these meat, poultry, seafood and vegetables have Clostridium botulinum which can form spores that can withstand boiling temperature. The spores can also grow in low acid foods which can produce toxins. The only way to destroy the spores is by exposing the food to 240 degrees temperature or even higher.

High acidic foods like fruits and properly picked vegetables have high content of acid which can prevent the spores from growing and producing deadly toxins.

Canning Equipment

Water bath canner

The water bath canner is a cooking pot with a lid and rack that prevents the jars from touching each other. The rack also allows the water to freely move around the jars. If the rack is not available, you can use clean dish towels and pack it in between the jars. The diameter of the canner should not be more than 4 inches of the diameter of the burner. Choose canners with flat bottom as much as possible.

Pressure canners

Pressure canners are heavy pots with lid that can trap the steam inside. The lid can also be fitted with a vent of weighted pressure gauge for safety reasons.

Jars

Mason and ball jars the designed for canning food. Avoid using jars from mayonnaise, baby food and pickle containers. Other jars may also not be appropriate since they are not heat treated.

There are a variety of sizes of jars which you can use. Pint and quart ball jars are more common than wide mouth top jars. These jars can also be used indefinitely as long as you store them properly.

Jar lids

Canning jars usually have a two piece sealing lid with rubber sealing compound on one side. The flat lid should only be used once but the band can be reused as long as it is clean.

Meat, chicken and seafood recipes

Beef stew

5 lb beef stew, cut into cubes

8 cups sliced carrots

3 cups chopped onion

1 tsp thyme

Water

1 tbsp oil of choice

3 cups chopped celery

2 tsp salt

½ tsp pepper

Makes 32 quarts

Prepare the pressure canner in advance. Heat the lids and jars in hot water until you are ready to use them. Simmer for few minutes then set aside. Heat a pan and cook the meat in oil. Add the vegetables. Sprinkle the seasoning and pour the hot water on top. Boil the stew then remove from heat.

Gently transfer the stew into the jars. Leave enough space on top. Make sure that there are no air bubbles by tapping the glass gently. Wipe the rim of the jar clean and fit the lid securely. Process the stew in the canner for 1 hour and 15 minutes. Take out the jar carefully then allow it to cool. Check the lid after a day. The lid should not flex up of down when pressed.

Chicken soup

4 quarts homemade chicken broth

1 cup chopped celery

1 cup chopped onion

1 clove garlic

4 cups chopped chicken

Salt and pepper to taste

2 cups carrots

Makes 4 quarts

Pour the broth in a pot then add the chopped chicken. Homemade broth makes the best chicken soup. Wash and drain the vegetables then chop it into small pieces. Add these to the stock pot. Season it with salt and pepper. Add the chopped garlic and stir. Remember that fresh herbs can get stronger in flavor when they are canned so if you want to add some into the soup remember to remove it before pouring into the jars. Pour the soup into the jar and place in the pressure canning for 1 and half hours.

Salmon or shad

2 lb salmon or shad

Water

Salt and pepper for seasoning

Makes 2 lb

Prepare the canner by heating the jars and lids in hot but not boiling water. Make sure to set the bands aside. Dissolve 1 cup of salt in water for the brine. Cut the fish into medium pieces. Soak it in the salt water for an hour then allow to drain. Gently place the fish into the jars. Leave at least 1 inch of space on top. Replace the lid on the jar then adjust the band until it is tight. Place the jars in the canner and process for 1 hour and 40 minutes.

Turkey and mixed vegetables

½ cup onions

½ cup almond flour

3 cups cooked turkey, diced

½ tsp salt

¼ tsp pepper

½ cup butter

6 cups chicken broth

3 cups frozen vegetables

2 tbsp parsley

Makes 5 jars

Cook the onions in a pan with butter until it is fragrant and soft. Add the flour and stir. Cook it for a minute. Stir it often to prevent lumps. Cook until the sauce is thick. Add the rest of the ingredients and heat it thoroughly. Remove from the heat. Allow to cool completely. Pour it into freezer jars then place the lid. Place in the freezer. This recipe can last for a year.

Vegetable recipes

Pickled asparagus

3 lb asparagus

2 ½ cups water

3 tsp mustard seeds

1 seeded and sliced lemon

2 ½ cups white vinegar

2 ½ tsp pickling salt

6 peeled garlic cloves

Makes 6 jars

Pour water into the canning pot and place on top of the stove. Wash the jars and lids and place in the water. Boil for 10 minutes or longer. Set it aside to cool. Pour the water, salt and vinegar in a pot to boil. Trim the asparagus and fit in the jar. Make sure that you also add one garlic clove and half teaspoon of mustard seed into each jar. Pack the asparagus tightly. Add a lemon slice in the jar. Pour the boiling vinegar into the jar and leave enough space on top. Wipe the rim and screw the lid. Use tongs to lower the jars into the boiling water bath. Boil for 10 minutes and cool at room temperature. Label the jar properly before storing.

Turkish fermented cabbage

4 lb cored and trimmed white head cabbage, shredded

3 tbsp minced garlic

3 tbsp Aleppo pepper

4 ½ cups water

6 tbsp salt

3 tbsp minced ginger

1 1.2 tsp sugar

Makes 2 ½ quarts

Shred the cabbage as fine as possible. Place it in a bowl then season with the salt. Place a plate on top and leave for 3 hours at room temperature. Rinse and drain the cabbage with cold water. Mix in the ginger, garlic, sugar and pepper. Pack the mixture into clean jars. Dissolve water into 4 ½ cups of cold water and pour this broth on top the jar. Screw the lid on top. For 10 days, you will have to stir the mixture with clean spoon. You can then place in the refrigerator and store for up to 6 months.

Pickled beets

5 medium red beets, trimmed

5 golden beets, trimmed

1 ½ tsp mustard seed

1 tsp whole allspice

¼ tsp whole clove

5 fresh bay leaves

1 ¼ tsp dry white wine

¼ tbsp sugar

2 tsp coriander seeds

¾ tsp dill seed

½ tsp fenugreek seeds

¼ tsp crushed red pepper

1 ¼ cups white wine vinegar

1 tbsp salt

Makes 2 quarts

Place the red beets in a saucepan and cover it slowly with water. Do the same for the golden beets. Bring the beets to a boil. Reduce to a simmer for 30 minutes. Peel the beets and cut into rounds. Transfer into containers. Stir the spices in a bowl and divide it evenly. Stir in the water, wine, sugar and salt in a pan. Boil then pour over the beets. Allow to cool completely and refrigerate for 10 hours. Serve at room temperature or cold.

Pickled dill carrots

4 lb carrots, sliced into sticks

5 tsp dill seeds

6 cups water

¼ cup pickling salt

5 garlic cloves

2 ½ cups vinegar

Makes 5 jars

Preheat the oven. Submerge your jars into hot water and bring to a simmer. Remember to remove the lid first. Remove the canners from the water and place in the oven. Place 1 tsp of dill and garlic into each jar. Pack with carrot sticks. Cover with hot brine but leave enough space on top. Screw the lids and place in a boiling pot of water for 10 minutes. Air bubbles should come out of the jars. Set it aside for a day.

Spiced pickled carrots

2 ¾ lb peeled carrots

1 cup water

2 tsp canning salt

8 garlic cloves

5 ½ cups white vinegar

2 cups sugar

2 tsp dill seed

14 tsp hot pepper flakes

Makes 4 jars

Wash and peel the carrots. Wash it again then set aside. Prepare the jars by submerging it in simmering water. Allow to cool before packing the jars with carrots. Mix the sugar, water, vinegar and salt in a saucepan then boil. Add the carrots and boil for another 10 minutes. Place the dill, pepper and garlic in each jar. Fill it with water. Wipe the lid before replacing the lid. Place the jars in boiling water for 15 minutes.

Pickled cauliflower

1 head cauliflower

4 tsp pumpkin seed

4 dried hot chilies

7 cups white vinegar

5 tbsp pickling salt

4 sunflower seed

4 tsp sesame seeds

2 tsp dried thyme

7 cups water

Makes 4 quarts

Pour water into a large pot. Cook the seeds in a pan until fragrant. Stir occasionally. Remove from the heat once you hear it pop. Cut the cauliflower into pieces and stir the stems as well. Divide the toasted spices into the jars. Fit the cauliflower into the jars. Boil the vinegar, water and salt. Wipe the rim of the jars before securing the lid. Submerge it in hot canner and process for 10 minutes then allow to cool on the counter.

Vietnamese carrot and radish pickle

3 cups white vinegar

2 tsp grated ginger

2 lb dense radish

3 cups water

2 lb carrots, thinly sliced

6 whole star anise

Makes 6 jars

Combine the vinegar, sugar, water and ginger in a pan. Boil over medium heat then stir to dissolve the sugar. Add the carrots and radish then stir to combine. Remove this from heat. Place the star anise into each jar. Pack the vegetables carefully and pour the hot liquid to cover the vegetables. Remove the air bubbles and place the lid. Boil a pot of water then submerge the jars for 10 minutes. Allow to cool before storing in a dark place.

Radish relish

2 cups distilled white vinegar

1 tbsp kosher salt

1 tbsp cumin seed

2 lb radish, shredded

2 inch knob ginger

1 tbsp whole coriander

1 tbsp yellow mustard seed

1 cup diced onion

2 minced garlic

Makes 4 jars

Combine the white vinegar, salt, whole coriander and cumin seeds in a pot and bring it to a boil. Add the remaining ingredients then boil again. Stir to ensure that the ingredients are well heated through. Remove it from the heat. Ladle the mixture into the jars and cover it with liquid. Leave enough space on top. Release the air bubbles. Wipe the rim clean before replacing the covers. Process it for 15 minutes. Set aside for a day before you store in a cool and dark space.

Jams, Jellies and Marmalades

Apple pie jam

4 cups apples, chopped

1 tsp cinnamon

¼ tsp ginger

1 cup stevia

1 tsp butter

1 ½ tsp lemon juice

¼ tsp nutmeg

4 cups natural raw honey

Makes 2 jars

Measure the apples and place in a saucepan. Add the butter, lemon juice and spices. Bring the mixture to a boil. Add the sugar to the pan and bring to a boil. Stir constantly for a minute. Remove it from the heat and skim off the foam. Ladle the mixture into the jars but ensure that you leave enough headspace. Replace the lid and submerge in hot water bath for 10 minutes.

Apple and earl grey almond jelly

3 ¼ lb Granny Smith apples

4 cups honey or stevia

3 ½ tbsp Earl Grey tea

6 ½ cups water plus more for the tea

2 tbsp lemon juice

¼ tsp almond extract

Makes 4 jars

Wash and drain the apples. Cut into quarters and place at the bottom of the pot. Cover with water and simmer at low heat. This will make the apples soft. Strain the mixture using layers of cheesecloth. Strain it again and pour the juice in the bowl. Place in the refrigerator overnight. Measure 4 ½ cups of the juice and add the lemon juice and sugar. Boil water for the tea and allow the tea bags to seep. Add the tea into the mixture and boil again. Remove this from heat. Add the almond extract. Pour the hot jelly into the jars and submerge into hot water. Process the jams for 5-10 minutes.

Banana jam

¼ cup fresh lime juice

1 ½ cups sugar

1 ½ tsp ground cinnamon

3 ½ cups diced ripe banana

½ cup water

Makes 1 jar

Chop the bananas into small pieces. Remember that overripe bananas tend to be sweeter so you can lessen the amount of sweetener. Combine the sugar and water in a pot then stir to dissolve. Bring to a boil. Add the banana mixture and simmer for 30 minutes or until it is thick. You have to keep stirring and mash the banana as you go. Add the cinnamon into the mixture and stir again. Remove from heat then allow it to cool. Scoop the jam into the jars and seal.

Banana and passion fruit jam

250 g bananas

230 g honey

50 g passion fruit pulp

Makes 2 jars

Mash the bananas in a bowl then mix it with the passion fruit and sweetener. Stir to combine then place in a saucepan. Heat it and stir constantly. Bring to a boil and remove the foam that may form on top. Remember to stir all the time. Continue to boil until the mixture is thick. Remove it from the heat. The jam may be a little thin while it is hot but will start to thicken as it cools off. Remove from the heat. Pour the jam into jars and secure the lids tightly. Unopened jams can be stored for 3 months. Consume the jam in a week after opening.

Money butter

5 medium ripe bananas

¼ cup coconut

3 tbsp lemon juice

20 oz crushed pineapple, not drained

3 cups stevia

Makes 2 jars

Bring a saucepan of water to boil. Chop the bananas and add to the pot. Combine with the remaining ingredients. Cook until it is thick. Stir constantly. Scoop the jams into the jars and replace with lid. Submerge it in hot water for 15 minutes.

Cranberry orange jelly

1 lb bag cranberries

Seat of 2 medium oranges

Pinch of salt

¼ tsp allspice

1 whole star anise

1 cup water

2/3 cup stevia

½ tsp cinnamon

10 whole cloves

Makes 4 jars

Stir the ingredients in a large pan over medium heat. Make sure that the cranberries are covered in water. Bring to a boil and simmer with the lid on. Cook for 10 minutes. You will start to hear the cranberries popping out of their skin. Reduce the heat and adjust the taste. Add more stevia if it is too sour. Cook for another 5 minutes. Pour in a jar and secure the lid tightly. Store in the refrigerator and use as necessary.

Blueberry jam

100 g bananas, mashed

230 g stevia

200 g blueberries

Juice from half lemon

Makes 1 cup

Rinse the berries and crush it with a fork. Place the mashed bananas, stevia, blueberries and lemon juice in a pan and mix well. Make sure to stir the mixture constantly with a wooden spoon. Bring to boil and remove any excess foam that floats on top. Continue to boil the mixture for 5 minutes until it becomes clear and thick. Remove it from heat then ladle into jars. Place on the lids and allow to cool. The jam can be stored for 3 months.

Blackberry jam

1 cup mashed berries

1 1/4 lemon juice

Half of apple, grated

½ cup stevia

Makes 1 jar

Add all of the ingredients in a saucepan and cook at medium heat for 10 minutes. Stir the mixture and allow the ingredients to fully incorporate. Reduce the heat and continue to cook for 20 minutes. The water will start to evaporate in 20 minutes. Cook until the bubbles forms on top. Pour the jam into sterilized containers. Store in the refrigerator after it has cooled.

Golden raspberry jam

2 cups stevia

1 1/3 lb golden raspberries

Juice of a lemon

Makes 2 jars

Remove any dirt from the raspberries without washing them. This way you can keep their fragrance. Discard any fruit that is moldy or mushy. Mix the sweetener, lemon juice and fruit. Boil then stir occasionally. Continue to cook at high temperature. Stir carefully. Return it to the pan and boil again. Remove the foam on top then set aside. Pour the mixture in the jars then refrigerate when it is cooled.

Pear preserves

6 cups peeled and cored pears

1 tbsp lemon juice

2 tsp ground all spice

4 cups stevia

1 cup water

2 tsp ground nutmeg

2 oz pectin

Makes 2 jars

Sterilize the jars in a pot of boiling water. Combine the lemon juice, fruit and water in a pan then simmer for 10 minutes. Add the pectin and bring to a boil. Stir in the sweetener then season with spices. Ladle into the jars and screw the lid. Process in hot water for 10 minutes.

Pie Fillings

Sweet black cherry pie filling

10 lb sweet black cherries, thawed in the refrigerator for a day

1/3 cup lemon juice

2 cups stevia

½ tsp ground cinnamon

Makes 5 jars

Place a colander on a large bowl then place the cherries on the colander. Cover with plastic and stir. Set aside until you have 7 cups of juice. Prepare the canner, lid and the canning jars. Combine the stevia and cinnamon in a bowl. Add the cherry juice. Place the pot over medium heat and boil. Remember to stir occasionally to prevent burning. Add the lemon and stir again. Add the cherries all at once. Stir again until it resumes boiling. Remove the pan from the heat. Scoop the filling into the jars and cover with water. Place in the canner over high heat. Bring to a boil then process the jars for 35 minutes. Place in a cooling rack to cool undisturbed.

Blackberry pie filling

6 quarts fresh blackberries

9 1/3 cups water

5 cups stevia

1 tsp cinnamon

½ cup lemon juice

Mix the cinnamon and sweetener in a large saucepan. Mix in the water and whisk to combine. Stir until it is thick enough. Heat until it boils. Add the lemon juice and boil for a minute and remember to stir constantly. You can add more water if you want to use this as a topping instead of a filling. Remove then add the berries. Stir then ladle into jars. Make sure to leave enough headspace. Process it in boiling water for 30 minutes before storing or using.

Peach blueberry pie filling

5 lb fully ripe peaches

6 cups fresh blueberries

1 1/3 cups tapioca starch

½ tsp ground cinnamon

2 ¼ cups water

3 ½ cups sugar

1 tsp grated fresh ginger

1/8 tsp ground nutmeg

¾ cup lemon juice

Makes 4 jars

Rinse the peaches and slice it in half. Submerge it in boiling water for 30 seconds until the skin cracks. Remove then rinse in cold water. Remove the pits and cut into slices. Wash and drain the blueberries. Heat the water in a Dutch oven and bring to a boil. Add the peaches and boil again. Boil for a minute and transfer the peaches into a bowl. Remove the liquid from the pot.

In the same pot, mix in the tapioca, cinnamon, sweetener and nutmeg. Stir in the water and set aside for 5 minutes to soften. Cook it over high heat and remember to stir occasionally. Add the lemon juice and stir. Add the fruits and stir to coat. Set it aside for 3 minutes then spoon the mixture into canning jars. Leave ½ inch headspace. Wipe the jars clean and process it in boiling canner for 30 minutes. Remove from the water and cool on the rack.

Canning Tips and Tricks

Extend the shelf life of your preserves

Canned preserves can last for 3 months to a year if left unopened. However, its lifespan is significantly reduced once it is opened since it is exposed to the air.

Use clean utensils every time you scoop into the jar. Using clean utensils can keep foreign microorganisms out of the preserves. Also, keep the lids tightly closed to prevent bacteria from entering. Eat preserves made with fruit butter first. Sugar is a preservative but since Paleo diet tries to use alternative such as honey and stevia, they don't last as long once opened so try to consume these canned preserves first.

Tips for making a good marmalade

Choose the fruit

Make sure that you choose fruit that has not been sprayed with any pesticide or preservatives. Locally grown fruits are also mostly recommended.

Taste and texture

Most marmalades use the whole fruit for the process. The fruit should not be soft before adding any sweetener and before processing it. You can do this by boiling the whole fruit or slice it into pieces before soaking it in hot water.

Ensuring set

Try to make marmalades in small batches in a wide a pan. The amount of pectin in fruits are usually enough to make your preserve.

How to be creative and still be safe

You can play around and experiment with different fruits to achieve different taste. Adding alcohol into your preserves can enhance its flavor. Try to do it in small amounts first before you increase the amount of ingredients. However, there are fruits which should be used with caution. Some fruits like figs, bananas, tomato and dates have different acidity levels so try to stick to the recipe as much as possible.

How to save runny jam

You will notice that there will be times where you will wind up with runny jams that have not set well. You should always give the canned preserve one to two days to set. If it still doesn't set after 2 days, you need to pour it back into a wide pot. Heat it and bring to a boil. Add one tablespoon of pectin and stir. Cook until the jam appears to thicken. Remove from the heat once it reaches your desired thickness. Pour the jam into jars and wipe the rims. Process it in boiling water for 10 minutes. Allow to cool.

How to prevent jar breakage

You can prevent your canning jars from breaking by not using metal utensils inside it. This is especially true if you are already trying to scoop the last remains of the jar. The metal scraping can cause small scratches that can lead to breakage later on.

You should also store the jars away from extreme temperature. Make sure that the jars are also hot before you pour hot preserves on the jar. Never submerge cold jars into the canner because it will break. Also, a gentle boil will prevent the jars from banging together and will prevent breakage. Lastly, you should not can jars that are only half full since this can make them prone to breakage.

How to store your canned jars

 Keep your canned jars out of direct sunlight since this can deteriorate your product. A cooler temperature is also more ideal. Although it is not advised that you keep them at freezing temperature, you should not store your jars near heaters and radiators. Keep the storage space accessible and do not place them in obscure areas where you are more likely to forget them.

Remove the ring once the jars are sealed and cooled. This can alert you if there has been any growth in the jars since this will dislodge the lid and let you know about the problem.

What to do if black scum forms outside the jars

Once you leave the jars to cool on the counter top, you may find black scum has formed at the rims. Your canned preserves are still good provided that the seal is intact. The black scum that you might see on the rim are pieces of jams that are trapped to the ring. It reacted to the metal and formed into the scum. You will just need to clean it off by wiping it with damp cloth. You can also soak it in water for few minutes until it becomes easy to scrub off with a towel. Check to ensure that the seal is still good before storing it.

How to throw away spoils

As a general rule, you should always throw away any home canned food if you have doubt about their safety. You might notice that the preserve turns into a different color or that the seal is not intact anymore.

Remember that low acid products like tomatoes should be discarded in a way that it will not be consumed by human or animal. Do not throw it on a composite or flush it down if you suspect that it harbors botulism. Place the jar into plastic sealable bags. Make sure to avoid skin contact as much as possible. Any towels that were used to clean the contaminated surface should also be discarded. Place this in the trash can and make sure that it is away from humans and pets. Only low acid foods can harbor botulism so these steps would not be necessary for fruit sauce, pickles and jams.

Importance of labeling jars

It can be difficult to locate a specific jar of preserves just by looking at it. A black berry jam can be similar to a strawberry preserve. Labeling your jars will also let you know the exact date when the canned good was made. Labeling is pretty simple. You can just use a marker to write on the lid or you can use a sticker paper and stick it to the jars. Be sure to place the date as well as the name of the good that you made.

Air bubbles in your jars

The bubbles from fruit sauces can be more difficult to remove than jams. As you pour the product into the jars, it is inevitable that some bubbles remain no matter how diligent you are at removing the bubbles as long as the jar was processed appropriately, you should not worry about the bubbles. The only time you should be worried is when the bubbles are moving to the top when you open it. This may indicate that the product is starting to ferment.

How to check the seal of the jars

One of the ways to know if your jams have been properly sealed is when you hear a ringing sound when you lock it in. You can also press down the lid and test if it flexes in other directions. If it does not move then it means that you have it sealed tight. You should also be able to lift the jar up while holding on to nothing but the lid.

Thank you again for downloading this book!

I hope you enjoyed reading about my book on how to can Paleo preserves.

Finally, if you enjoyed this book, please take the time to share your thoughts and **post a review on Amazon**. It'd be greatly appreciated!

Thank you!

Next Steps

- Write me an honest review about the book – I truly value your opinion and thoughts and I will incorporate them into my next book, which is already underway.

Leave your review of my book here: DIRECT LINK TO REVIEW FOR YOUR BOOK

Made in the USA
Middletown, DE
03 August 2022